FIREFLIES

FIREFLIES

by Bernice Kohn

illustrated by Erwin Schachner

LIBRARY EDITION 1970
RESPONSIVE ENVIRONMENTS CORP.
Englewood Cliffs, N.J. 07632

Prentice-Hall, Inc., Englewood Cliffs, N.J.

For G. D. W.

Third printing...... March, 1968

Fireflies by Bernice Kohn

Library of Congress Catalog Card Number: 66-22087

Printed in the United States of America

J 31753

PRENTICE-HALL INTERNATIONAL, INC., *London*
PRENTICE-HALL OF AUSTRALIA, PTY. LTD., *Sydney*
PRENTICE-HALL OF CANADA, LTD., *Toronto*
PRENTICE-HALL OF INDIA PRIVATE LTD., *New Delhi*
PRENTICE-HALL OF JAPAN, INC., *Tokyo*

Contents

1.

Little Stars

Fluttering white-fire insects.
Wavering small-fire beasts!
Wave little stars about my bed!
Weave little stars into my sleep!

From an
Ojibway Indian chant.

As dusk falls on a summer night, the garden starts to sparkle with tiny bursts of light. The fireflies have begun to flash their twinkling lamps. They continue until the sun has truly set and heavy darkness settles down. Then, except for a stay-up-late straggler or two, the fireflies turn off their lights and the lovely display is over.

Have you ever looked at a firefly very closely? There are many different kinds in the United States, but the most common fireflies are usually between a quarter of an inch and three-quarters of an inch long. They are long, slender and rather flat. Their color ranges from brown to dusty black. There are often yellow margins or stripes on the body and sometimes a bit of red.

To understand the general anatomy of a fire-fly, it is useful to know something about its relatives and to see just where fireflies fit into the large animal kingdom.

There are so many different kinds of animals that scientists divide them into *phyla,* the Greek word for tribes. There are nineteen phyla in all and the largest is called *Arthropoda* (Ar-THROP-o-da). Fireflies belong to this phylum—and so do eighty percent of all the other animals in the world!

Arthropoda, in Greek, means *joint-foot,* and every creature in the phylum has jointed legs. They also have some other things in common. They have no bones inside their bodies at all. Instead, they have a hard outer covering called an *exoskeleton.* Exo means outside. The body, with its exoskeleton, is made up of distinct sections.

All of these requirements are met by such different animals as crabs, shrimp and centipedes.

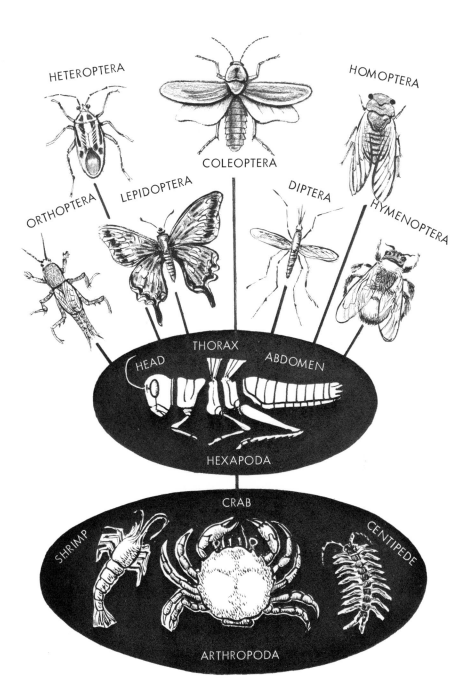

HETEROPTERA

COLEOPTERA

HOMOPTERA

ORTHOPTERA

LEPIDOPTERA

DIPTERA

HYMENOPTERA

HEAD

THORAX

ABDOMEN

HEXAPODA

CRAB

SHRIMP

CENTIPEDE

ARTHROPODA

You can see that some more divisions are needed before we get down to fireflies.

And so the phylum is divided into thirteen classes. One of them is *Hexapoda* (Hex-AP-o-da), or *Insecta,* and it includes all of the insects.

Hexapoda comes from two Latin words which mean *six* and *feet.* All insects, including fireflies, of course, have six legs. In addition, all insects breathe air. They have three main body parts: a head, a thorax and an abdomen. They usually have one or two pairs of wings when they are adults.

The class Hexapoda includes close to a million different kinds of insects and each one passes through several stages—egg, larva or nymph, pupa and adult. Surely some more dividing is in order. And order is just the right word. The different groups of insects are called *orders* and the one that fireflies belong to is the order *Coleoptera* (Co-lee-OP-te-ra), or beetles.

Did you think that the firefly was a beetle? Its name says it is a fly but it most definitely is *not* a fly. It is a true beetle.

Beetles have chewing jaws. They generally have two pairs of wings, one over the other. The

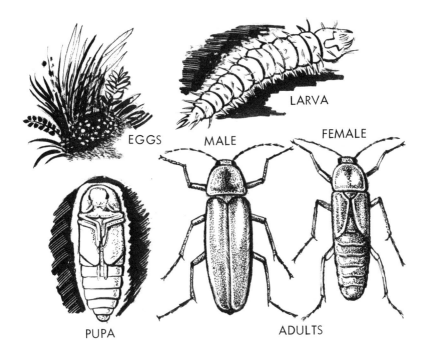

EGGS   LARVA   MALE   FEMALE   PUPA   ADULTS

outer wings are hard and stiff and form a cover for the delicate, gauzy underwings. When at rest, a beetle's wing covers fit so closely down the back that the seam is almost invisible. Sometimes you cannot tell that there are wings there at all until the insect suddenly takes to the air.

Beetles have eyes that are made up of many different lenses. Each one has a number of sides and surfaces like a finely cut diamond with many facets. They are called *compound* eyes and can see in many directions at once. There is one kind

5

of male firefly that has 2,500 separate lenses in its eye!

All beetles, including fireflies, have a pair of feelers, or antennae, on their heads. These are very sensitive and help the beetle to see, smell, feel and hear.

Among the vast number of beetles, fireflies belong to a special family called *Lampyridae* (Lam-PIR-i-dye). There are 1,500 different kinds of Lampyridae and more than half of them are found in the Americas. There are about sixty kinds of fireflies in the United States alone. They occur in all parts of the country except the far west.

Before a firefly becomes the twinkling insect that you know, it has to pass through a number of stages called *instars*. But the beginning is an egg. Let's start, as the firefly does, with an egg, and see how the insect grows.

2.

Early Stages

A mother firefly lays a great many eggs, perhaps one hundred, two hundred or even more. They may land on the ground, a twig or on a blade of grass. In the United States, this process takes place in late June or early July.

The mother doesn't even look to see where the eggs are. She has done her job. She goes on her way and has no further interest in her children.

From the very moment that they appear, the eggs glow with a soft light. After about twenty-six days, almost all of the eggs hatch and the tiny worm-like larvae appear. These are called glowworms. The glowworms do not fare as well as the eggs. Large numbers of them are killed by heavy rains and many others are eaten by larger insects such as ground beetles.

The glowworm is rather flat. It has a small, narrow head with very strong, curved jaws. The jaws are important because the glowworm's chief interest is food.

While they eat cutworms and earthworms, glowworms particularly favor snails and slugs. They seek them out in damp places. If you want to look for glowworms, a good place to find them is under a pile of damp, fallen leaves. The larvae are quiet during the day but they get busy at nightfall when they begin to search for food.

It doesn't seem possible that a tiny, soft-bodied little glowworm can capture and devour a big, fat snail, but it *is* possible and it happens all the time. As a matter of fact, glowworms are such enormous eaters that they are considered valuable in farming areas where snails and slugs are a danger to crops.

The secret of the glowworm's success is its ability to inject its prey with a special fluid. As soon as the snail has received a "shot" of the fluid, it acts sleepy and tired. Very soon, it is completely paralyzed and can do nothing in order to fight or escape. The fluid does even more. It begins to soften the snail's flesh. It changes the rather solid,

rubbery snail into a soft, pulpy mass that the glowworm can eat and digest.

The glowworm goes on glowing and eating for a period of from one to two years. During cold weather, it crawls under a stone. Or, it may make itself a hollowed-out cell underneath the surface of the soil. All this time, the glowworm grows larger and larger. When its skin becomes too small, the glowworm sheds it and a new, larger skin takes its place. This *molting* takes place several times.

The next stage is the pupa. This is a halfway stage between larva and adult. The pupa stays underground or in a small earthen chamber above ground for several weeks. This is a time of resting and during it the pupa grows its wings, its markings, and everything it needs to be a complete firefly. When it leaves its hiding place it is an adult.

3.

The Adult Firefly

One of the amazing things about an adult firefly is that it never eats. It loses its appetite after the pupa stage and doesn't touch food again. It does take some moisture from dew and from the leaves of plants. Naturally, an animal that doesn't eat cannot live for a very long time. The life span of the adult firefly is usually about three weeks.

All adult male fireflies have wings. The females have them too, *except in one species.* These wingless females are called glowworms even when they are adults. This is unfortunately confusing, but you just have to remember that a glowworm is either a firefly larva, male or female, or an adult female without wings.

The first thing that comes to mind when we think of fireflies is a flashing light. Adult fireflies

can turn their lights on and off at will. It is generally thought that the flashing lights are used as mating signals. Naturalists have watched one particular species, *Photinus pyralis* (Fo-TEEN-us pyr-A-lis). They found that both males and females crawl out of the grass at nightfall. The male flies back and forth and flashes his light every few seconds. The female doesn't fly but rests on a tuft of grass or some other object that is low in height. She flashes *her* light only in answer to a male signal. The male continues to flash, the female continues to answer. Finally, the male sees the answering light. Flashing a few more times to make sure he has his bearings, the male flies straight toward the female beacon. Incidentally, it is interesting to note that most male fireflies have larger eyes and better vision than the females because they must be able to see the females' flashes which are not as bright as the males'. The extra large eyes enable the male to spot every flash no matter how feeble!

The famous naturalist, JEAN HENRI FABRE, did some experiments with a cageful of adult (female) glowworms. He wanted to see if anything could make them turn out their lights. First,

HENRI FABRE

Fabre fired a gun right next to the cage. It made a frightful noise but the glowing lights never blinked. Then he sprinkled the insects with cold water and finally blew smoke into the cage. In a few cases, the lights wavered for a second or two but then went on as bright as ever. It seems as if the lady glowworm won't let anything in-

15

terfere with her signal light—just in case a gentleman happens to be passing by.

Fabre also made another interesting observation. The adult glowworm has her light on the underside of her abdomen. If she remained flat on the ground, the light would be hard to see from the air. But Miss Glowworm takes care of that. She climbs to the top of a blade of grass and proceeds to turn and twist. She makes sure that her light shines in all directions, just like the searchlight at an airport.

In tropical countries the fireflies are often very large and adorned with different colored lights. The firebeetle of Panama (not a true firefly, but a light-producing beetle) is more than an inch long. It has a pair of brilliant green "headlights." Their light is so powerful that just a few of the beetles in a jar make a light that is good enough to read by. When they fly, the firebeetles sport flickering yellow lights on the underside of their bodies. Ladies often catch these fireflies and wrap them in little pieces of net. They fasten them like jewels to their hair or dresses.

In South America, there is a wingless firefly that is known as the railroad worm. The name is

easy to understand. This insect has a red head-light and eleven pairs of green lights along the sides of its body! Railroad worms are often captured and placed in little cages of bamboo, pottery or grass. The cages are then hung indoors as decorations or to provide soft, romantic lighting.

In Japan, many people keep busy during May and June catching and selling fireflies. There is a big demand for fireflies since they are put into little cages and used to decorate restaurants and gardens.

On Honshu Island near the town of Uji, the firefly collectors have a very special way of doing their work. They shake the trees and as the beetles fall out the collectors grab them with their hands. When their hands are full, they store the beetles in their mouths while they fill their hands again.

In the West Indies it is common to use fireflies for lanterns indoors or out. When the West Indians go hunting or fishing at night they do not want to lose each other in the dark. They imprison fireflies in strips of net and fasten them around their ankles and wrists.

4.

Signal Lights

The most common firefly light is greenish-yellow, but it is by no means always that color. The light may range from a bluish-green all the way to an orange-red.

The whole pattern of flashes varies, too. Experiments have shown that some fireflies flash more often in hot weather. One particular kind of firefly flashed about eight times a minute at a temperature of 70° Fahrenheit. When the temperature went up to 83.4° Fahrenheit, the fireflies flashed more often than fifteen times a minute.

Different varieties begin their flashing at different times after sunset. They do not know what time it is, of course, but they start when there is a certain degree of darkness. Often, storm clouds,

which cause early darkness, will start the fireflies flashing much earlier than usual.

Fireflies have different "codes" for signaling, too. Some use a certain number of flashes per minute; some fly in such a way that the lights seem to bob and shimmer in the air and some flash on and off signals—they wink and blink in their own pattern. At times the lights start near the ground and seem to float upward until they cannot be seen any longer. There are all sorts of combinations of variations in the color of the

light, the brightness, the number of flashes, the pause between flashes and the length of time the light stays on. Each species of firefly knows its own code and each answers only its own kind!

Certain fireflies have very special kinds of signals. Some people have observed a large number of fireflies all flashing at exactly the same time. This is called *synchronous* (SIN-kro-nus) flashing . The English word synchronous comes from two Greek words, *syn* which means same and *chronos,* time.

There have been a number of explanations of synchronous flashing and we do not know which one is the true one. The first known report of such flashing appeared in 1727. It was published in Englebert Kaempfert's *The History of Japan.* Kaempfert described a scene (not in Japan, as you would think, but along a river bank in Thailand!). He saw a dense mass of fireflies stretching for a quarter of a mile and all blinking on and off exactly together.

There have been other such reports and dozens of different explanations. DR. JOHN BONNER BUCK of Johns Hopkins University in Maryland, was interested in all the explanations of synchronous flashing. In 1938, he made a study of them. The main ones were:

1. It doesn't really happen but is only imagined by the observer.

2. It is seen because the observer's eyelids twitch.

3. It is accidental.

4. It has "something" to do with the sap of the tree that the insects rest on.

5. It is caused by puffs of wind.

6. It is caused by special conditions of temperature, humidity, air currents, darkness.

7. It is caused by crowding of fireflies, sympathy, or a sense of rhythm.

8. It is caused by the back-and-forth loss and recovery of "some battery-like mechanism."

9. There is a leader and all the others follow him as if he were an orchestra conductor.

10. One male flash may get an answer from thousands of females—all at exactly the same time.

As you can see, there are many possibilities but no real answer. If the answer is ever found, it will add much to our knowledge of fireflies.

The great chorus of flashes that come all at once occurs mostly in the tropics. Actually, only a few Americans have ever seen such a display. It is not very likely that you ever will. Most of the firefly lights that you see will flash and twinkle here and there. Just as the lights start at different times, they end at different times, too. Each insect continues to flash until he has found a mate. As soon as he has, he doesn't need to signal any longer. The lights grow fewer and fewer and after several hours there are hardly any to be seen.

If you would like to learn something about the signal lights of your neighborhood fireflies, here is an experiment you can try. It will show you how the fireflies respond to changes in temperature.

It is easy to catch a firefly with your hands. When you have caught one put it into a covered jar. A couple of holes punched in the lid will let in air. As adult fireflies do not eat you do not have to worry about food.

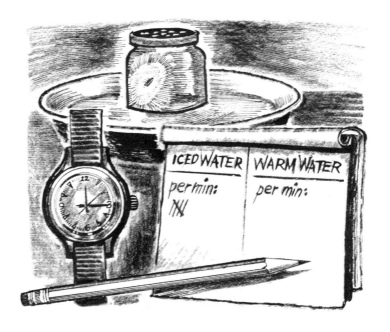

Since you only would be likely to catch a fire-fly that was flashing, he should continue to flash in the jar—if you conduct your experiment in a darkened room. Using a watch with a second hand, notice how often the flashes come. See how long each flash lasts and how bright it is.

Now put the jar into iced water. After a few minutes time the flashes again. They will probably occur less often, last a shorter time and give less light.

After you have jotted down a record, put the jar into warm water. When the firefly has had a chance to warm up, make your observations again. Depending on the temperature, you may get even faster and brighter flashes than you did the first time.

As soon as you have finished the experiment, let the firefly go. If you keep it too long it will die.

5.

Living Light

Light that is made by a living thing is called *bioluminescence. Bio* comes from the Greek word for life and *luminescence* from the Latin word for light.

Fireflies are not the only producers of bioluminescence. Many sea creatures, certain plants, other insects and a number of bacteria all give light.

Long, long ago, people noticed that foods like meat or fish that had been kept too long, began to glow with a ghostly light. So did decayed wood, old potatoes or fruit. Even cheese was seen to glow in the dark!

Way back in 1668, ROBERT BOYLE discovered that if he put a piece of spoiled meat in a jar and used a pump to remove all the air in the

jar, the light went out. No one had ever heard of oxygen in 1668 but we now know that there can be no bioluminescence without it. The spoiled meat stopped glowing because, when the air was removed, the meat had no oxygen.

Firefly lights need oxygen, too. There are two theories about how it is used. One is that it is just released by a reaction between nerves and muscles. The second theory is a little more complicated. It is claimed that each firefly has an elaborate network of oxygen pipes and every pipe has a tiny valve that works like a water faucet. Fireflies control their flashes by means of their nervous systems. When the firefly opens a valve it lets in more oxygen and the light is bright. When the firefly closes the valve, it lets in less oxygen and the light is dim. When the valve is completely closed, there is no oxygen and the light goes out.

Air was the first clue to the origin of bioluminescence. The second clue came in 1742 Henry Baker wrote a book entitled *The Microscope Made Easy.* In it, Baker suggested that the mysterious light might come from "tiny animals." Baker was right. The light of spoiled food *does* come from tiny organisms—now we call them *bacteria.*

But even after Baker's discovery, it was a long time before man began to find out anything more about bioluminescence. In 1887, a French physiologist, RAPHAEL DUBOIS, set out to discover the source of living light.

Dubois selected a light-giving clam, *Pholas dactylus* (FO-las DAC-ti-lus), and chopped it up. He soaked the chopped clam in cold water then drained off the water. The water glowed for a little while and then it stopped. Next, Dubois soaked some clams in hot water and that water did not glow. But when he mixed the hot water *with* the cold, the mixture *did* glow.

What had happened was this. With the cold water wash, Dubois had soaked out a substance which he called *luciferase* for Lucifer, the Roman god who was the bearer of light. The hot water destroyed the luciferase, but it soaked out another ingredient that must be present in order for luciferase to glow. Dubois named this ingredient *luciferin.*

Now we know that for light to be produced by a living thing we must have oxygen, luciferase and luciferin. But there is still another necessary ingredient. A modern scientist, Dr. William Mc-Elroy of Johns Hopkins University devoted himself to the study of bioluminescence. He found that, for fireflies, a chemical known at ATP was necessary, too. No matter how much oxygen, luciferin and luciferase, if there is not any ATP there is not any light.

Along with the knowledge of the "ingredients" of bioluminescence came other knowledge. It was discovered that living light was not produced by bacteria alone, as had been thought at first. Bacteria do account for the light given off by decaying foods, especially those which come from animals. Bacteria also make the light in certain live fish and squid. But light is actually *produced* by many other creatures of the sea without the aid of bacteria. Light is also manufactured by certain plants, earthworms and insects—including, of course, fireflies. For firefly light, oxygen, luciferin and luciferase, as well as ATP *must* be present.

This is not a problem because ATP is found in all living things. It turns up in all plants, all animals and even in those blobs of microscopic life which are so tiny they cannot properly be called either plant or animal.

Without ATP no plant can grow, no animal can digest food, no heart can beat, no lung can breathe. It is not surprising that ATP is needed for bioluminescence. It contains some phosphate as well as some nitrogen, a gas that is present in the air and an element that is necessary for plant growth. Adenine (AD-en-een), one of the ingredients in tea, and a pinch or two of sugar are other components of ATP.

Since it is known that wherever there is life there must be ATP, it is possible to use one to find out about the other. With this idea in mind, scientists have begun to use fireflies in a fascinating experiment.

Man has always wondered just how far out in space any form of life exists. There have been many efforts to find out. Balloons have been sent aloft to see how high they could go and still capture bits of life in the form of floating mold spores and pollens. Now, NASA, our space agen-

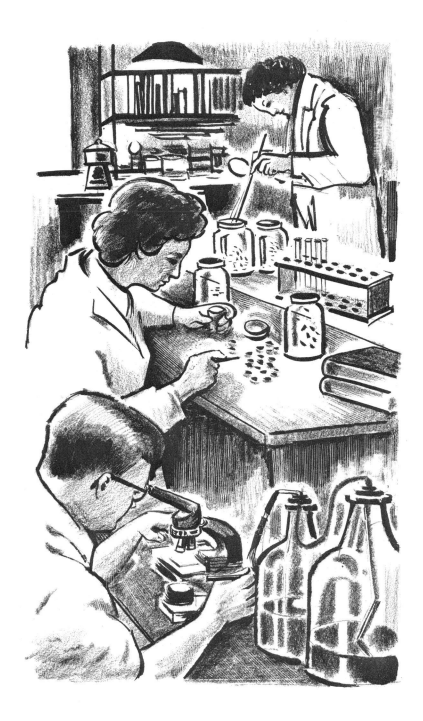

cy, has elaborate projects under way to land men and instruments on far away planets. The question everyone is most eager to settle is whether or not there is life on those planets.

This is where ATP comes into the picture. Scientists, with the help of thousands of school children, have been collecting fireflies. The scientists are planning to extract the fireflies' luciferin and luciferase and mix them with oxygen but *not* with ATP. As you know, this combination will not make any light. The mixture will then be flown far out into space. Wherever there is any life there is a chance that the chemicals will pick up a tiny speck of ATP. If they do, the mixture will begin to glow! That tiny ray of light will be enough to trigger delicate instruments that will radio the news back to earth.

It sounds a trifle fantastic, but, if you stretch your imagination just a bit, you can see that it might be fireflies that finally tell us whether or not there is life on distant planets.

6.

Cold Light

Sit in the sunlight and you feel warm. Sit in it too long and you may get burned. Build a camp fire and you cannot stay too close because it is hot. Turn on an electric light and you can feel the heat of the bulb with your hand.

It always takes some kind of energy to make light. The energy may come from burning fuel, from chemicals or from electricity. In any case, only a small part of the energy that is put into the job ever gets turned into light. The sun changes only about a third of its energy into light. The rest is given off as heat, invisible rays and gases.

An incandescent lamp changes from five to ten percent of its energy into light. Most of the energy is changed into heat. A fluorescent lamp does somewhat better. About twenty percent of its electrical energy turns into light.

If you held your hand over a candle flame, your hand would get very hot. It takes thousands of fireflies all aglow at the same time to give as much light as a candle. But, if you were to hold your hand over the fireflies you would feel nothing—firefly light is completely cold! It wastes no energy whatsoever in heat.

Scientists constantly struggle for better *efficiency,* or less waste of energy, in producing light. Gaslight was an improvement over oil lamps, electric lights were an improvement over gaslight. But with all the improvements, we are a long way from the remarkable cold light of the firefly. The great efficiency of cold light is one of its mysteries. Another, is why it was developed in the first place.

As you know, almost every organ in a living creature has a job to do. If it hasn't, you can be sure that it once did and the changes that take place in evolution just haven't gotten rid of it yet. Modern man's appendix is not important to him now, but millions of years ago it was. Since

the appendix now serves little or no purpose, it will probably grow smaller and smaller and in time it will disappear altogether.

This "purpose-for-everything" theory leads us to wonder about firefly light. We have learned that fireflies use their lights as mating signals but was that the original purpose of the light?

Bioluminescence is produced only by the so-called *lower forms of life.* They include certain insects, worms, fish, clams, bacteria and toad-stools. No reptile, bird, mammal or amphibian can make light. It would seem that the ability to do so was left way back on a low rung of the evolutionary ladder.

Some scientists, chief among them Dr. WILLIAM McELROY, have reached the following conclusion: Millions and millions of years ago, long before there was any life, there was no oxygen-containing air. There was, instead, a heavy mixture of poisonous gases. Later, the atmosphere cleared and air began to take the place of the other gases.

This took a long time. During the change-over period, the first single-celled living things began to appear. Oxygen was a poison to them (even though they needed to use a certain amount of it in order to change and grow). But they had to remove it from their systems at once before it killed them. These primitive creatures learned to get rid of some of the oxygen in their systems by combining it with hydrogen—thus producing water. They eliminated the rest of the "poisonous" oxygen by making light with it. Actually, they flashed their lights in order to remain alive!

Dr. McElroy's theory may give us some of the answers to the riddle of bioluminescence. Luminous bacteria never turn off their lights. They do

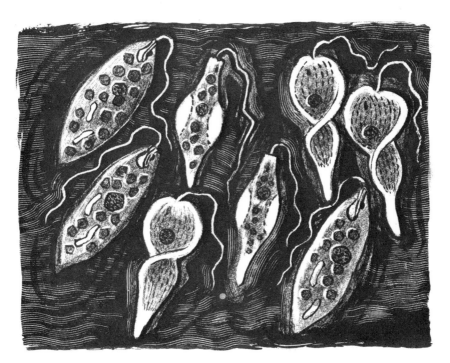

not seem to use flashes to attract mates nor to frighten enemies away. No one has ever understood what the light was for—now we have an idea. It is very possible that bacteria, like their ancient ancestors, *still* use light production as a means of getting rid of unwanted oxygen.

Fireflies, far-removed from their ancient one-celled ancestors, have never lost their ability to make light. But its original purpose has been lost. Fireflies do not have to get rid of oxygen. Instead, they use their flashing lights to signal each other on dusky summer evenings.

7.

Superstitions and Legends

Fireflies were probably seen by the very earliest peoples, and surely their fire must have been thought a kind of magic. The mystery of the light gave rise to many superstitions in different parts of the world.

Some people believe that if "fire" from a firefly gets into your eye you will lose the sight in the eye. And, if a firefly comes into your home, on the following day there will either be one person more or one person less in the house. Or, if a firefly comes into your home you will soon receive a visit from an old friend.

In some places, fireflies play a part in strange customs. On the Indonesian island of Nias, people fear that when a man is sick his soul may escape. If it does, the man will die. To prevent

this, a sorcerer sits watch beside the sick man's
bed. He is certain that he can see the soul escape
because it takes the form of a firefly. However,
the sick man's family cannot argue when the sorcerer says that the soul has gone because a "soul"
firefly is supposed to be invisible to everyone
except the sorcerer! The sorcerer runs outside,
probably dashes about a good bit, then "catches"

the invisible firefly. He wraps it in a cloth and places it on the patient's forehead. The man, having been given back his soul, is now supposed to get better.

There is a story often told of a cave in New Zealand which glows with a strange, mysterious light. For a long time, people believed that the glow was "magic" until it was discovered that

the walls and ceiling of the cave were completely covered with glowworms.

And there is even a story, which may or may not be true, about a doctor somewhere in the tropics. He had to perform an emergency operation and just as he was getting ready to begin there was a power failure and the lights went out. You guessed it—everyone ran out to collect fireflies and the good doctor saved a life by the light of the flashing jars!

Some of the earliest writings mention fireflies. A Chinese book, the *Shih Ching*, written about 3,000 years ago, has a line which has been translated to read, "Glowing intermittently are the fireflies."

And there is a famous story about a poor Chinese student who lived almost 2,000 years ago. Ch'e Yin was too poor to buy oil for his lamp. Instead, he collected fireflies and used their glow to study his books at night.

Fireflies figure in the writings of ancient India, Greece at the time of Christ, and many other countries. They are not mentioned in the Bible—most likely because fireflies like moist places and the Bible lands were very dry.

The North American Indians were observant
and appreciative of fireflies as they were of everything in nature. In his great poem, *The Song of
Hiawatha,* Henry Wadsworth Longfellow tells us:

> At the door on summer evenings
> Sat the little Hiawatha;
> . . . Saw the fire-fly, Wah-wah-taysee,
> Flitting through the dusk of evening,
> With the twinkle of its candle
> Lighting up the brakes and bushes,
> And he sang the song of children,
> Sang the song Nokomis taught him:
> "Wah-wah-taysee, little fire-fly,
> Little, flitting, white-fire insect,
> Little, dancing, white-fire creature,
> Light me with your little candle,
> Ere upon my bed I lay me,
> Ere in sleep I close my eyelids!"

One of the saddest of all firefly legends is from
China. It goes like this:

Once upon a time, there lived a very happy
family. There was a mother, a father and a son.
They dwelt in peace and harmony until one sad
day, the mother fell ill and died. The father was
very lonely and after a while he decided to marry
again. But alas, the woman he wed was not at all
like his first wife. Although she appeared for a
time to be a kindly person, she was really mean
and cruel. She disliked her stepson and seized
upon any excuse to give him a beating. The
poor little boy was terrified lest he displease this
dreadful woman.

48

One day, the stepmother gave the boy a few coppers and sent him across the mountain to the village to buy some peanut oil.

"Hurry back," she said, "and mind that you bring the oil."

The boy hurried as fast as he could, but when he reached the village, he discovered that the coppers were gone from his pocket. He didn't dare to return home without the oil, so he decided to look for the money. The boy searched and searched and after a while it grew dark. He still continued to hunt for the lost coppers and while he did so, a storm came up.

Now it was impossible to see a thing. The boy grew confused and lost his way. He stumbled through the forest until he fell into a stream and was drowned.

But so strong was his fear of his cruel step-mother that even in death that fear did not leave him. His spirit said over and over again, "I must find my coppers. I must find my coppers." And, the legend tells us, you can see the spirit of that little boy today. It is the firefly, its lamp held high, searching, searching everywhere for the coppers that were lost.

There are many fireflies in Japanese folklore, too. One old Japanese legend explains that fireflies are the ghosts of brave warriors who gave up their lives for their country.

In story, in history, in science, in art, fireflies have always stimulated man's imagination. The secret of their cold and beautiful light has mystified mankind since the dawn of civilization. Although we now have many clues to the workings of bioluminescence, scientists of today and tomorrow still have much to learn about—and from—the twinkling firefly.

Glossary

Arthropoda

The phylum that contains more species than any other in the animal kingdom. They include crabs, insects, spiders, centipedes and others. The classes belonging to phylum Arthropoda are: *Trilobita, Crustacea, Myriopoda, Arachnida* and *Insecta* (*Hexapoda*).

ATP

An abbreviation for adenosine triphosphate.

Bacteria

Microscopic single-celled organisms. There are many species of bacteria. Most of them are helpful to man, some are harmful.

Bioluminescence

The production of light by living organisms.

Class

A subdivision of a phylum. A class consists of one order or a number of similar orders.

Coleoptera

Beetles. A very large order of insects.

Exoskeleton

A hard covering on the outside of the body in place of internal bone structure.

Hexapoda or *Insecta*

The class of Arthropoda which includes springtails, silverfish, cockroaches, earwigs, termites, flies, greenflies, bugs, lice, fleas, butterflies, beetles, bees and ants. Most insects live on land and breathe air by means of tracheae. They have one pair of antennae, three pairs of legs and three distinct body parts: head, thorax and abdomen. Most insects have wings.

Instar

A stage between two molts in the larval development of an insect.

Lampyridae

A family of the order Coleoptera.

Larva

The form in which some animals hatch from the egg. It is capable of fending for itself but is quite different from the mature adult. The caterpillar is the larva of the butterfly.

Molting or *ecdysis*

In arthropoda, the periodic shedding of the skin as the animal grows.

Nymph

A young stage of certain insects. It resembles the adult but is sexually immature. It is either wingless or has wings that are only partly developed.

Order

A subdivision of a class. An order consists of one family or a number of similar families.

Phylum

One of the major groups used in classifying animals. It consists of one class or a number of similar classes.

Pupa or *chrysalis*
A stage between pupa and adult of some insects. Motion and feeding stop but great changes take place.

Index

595.7
K

c.1

Kohn, Bernice
Fireflies

595.7
K

c.1

Kohn, Bernice

AUTHOR

Fireflies

TITLE

DATE DUE	BORROWER'S NAME	ROOM NUMBER
3/12/82	Woody	
FEB. 4	Micah	
9-21	Garrett	3
93-94		